D0931785

Mapping the Continents

Mapping Asia

Paul Rockett

with artwork by Mark Ruffle

Crabtree Publishing Company

www.crabtreebooks.com

Crabtree Publishing Company
www.crabtreebooks.com
1-800-387-7650

Published in Canada
616 Welland Ave.
St. Catharines, ON
L2M 5V6

Published in the United States
PMB 59051, 350 Fifth Ave.
59th Floor,
New York, NY

Published in 2017 by CRABTREE PUBLISHING COMPANY.

First published in 2016 by The Watts Publishing Group (An imprint of Hachette Children's Group)
Copyright © The Watts Publishing Group 2016

Author: Paul Rockett

Editorial director: Kathy Middleton

Editors: Adrian Cole, and Ellen Rodger

Proofreader: Wendy Scavuzzo

Series design and illustration:
   Mark Ruffle, www.rufflebrothers.com

Prepress technician: Katherine Berti

Print and production coordinator: Katherine Berti

Printed in Canada/072016/PB20160525

Picture credits:
David Copeman/Alamy: 24cl; Bernardo Erti/Dreamstime: 19br; Kojin/Shutterstock: 17bl; Richard Powers/Corbis: 25tl; Rex/Shutterstock: 23tl; Lena Serditova/Shutterstock: 27c; Travel mania/Shutterstock: 21tl; Vincentstthomas/Dreamstime: 23b; Wikimedia Commons: 6-7; World History Archive/Superstock: 5cl; Zurijeta/Shutterstock: 27t.

Every attempt has been made to clear copyright. Should there by any inadvertent omission please apply to the publisher for rectification.

Library and Archives Canada Cataloguing in Publication

Rockett, Paul, author
        Mapping Asia / Paul Rockett.

(Mapping the continents)
Includes index.
Issued in print and electronic formats.
ISBN 978-0-7787-2613-5 (hardback).--
ISBN 978-0-7787-2619-7 (paperback).--
ISBN 978-1-4271-1780-9 (html)

        1. Asia--Juvenile literature. 2. Cartography--Asia--Juvenile literature. 3. Asia--Geography--Juvenile literature. 4. Asia--Description and travel--Juvenile literature. 5. Asia--Maps--Juvenile literature.
I. Title.

DS5.R63 2016   j915   C2016-902652-3
                                                        C2016-902653-1

Library of Congress Cataloging-in-Publication Data

Names: Rockett, Paul, author.
Title: Mapping Asia / Paul Rockett.
Description: New York, New York : Crabtree Publishing Company, 2017. |
Series: Mapping the continents | Includes index. |
Identifiers: LCCN 2016016673 (print) | LCCN 2016024420 (ebook) |
ISBN 9780778726135 (reinforced library binding) |
ISBN 9780778726197 (pbk.) |
ISBN 9781427117809 (electronic HTML)
Subjects: LCSH: Asia--Juvenile literature. | Cartography--Asia--Juvenile
   literature. | Asia--Geography--Juvenile literature. | Asia--Description
   and travel--Juvenile literature.
Classification: LCC DS5 .R59 2017 (print) | LCC DS5 (ebook) |
DDC 915--dc23
LC record available at https://lccn.loc.gov/2016016673

Contents

Where is Asia?

ASIA

Asia is the largest continent in the world. Its giant landmass borders Africa and Europe to the west and the Pacific Ocean to the east, where the continent is made up of thousands of islands.

Landmass

Asia covers just under one third of all the land on Earth.

Europe

Africa

ASIA

Pacific
Ocean

Indian
Ocean

Locating Asia

We can describe the position of Asia in relation to the areas of land and water that surround it, as well as by using the points on a compass.

- Asia is east of Europe
- Asia is northeast of Africa
- Asia is north of the Indian Ocean
- Asia is west of the Pacific Ocean

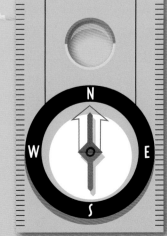

N

W   E

S

4

Making the continent even larger

Continents are divided by natural features, such as mountain ranges or seas. Some geographers define a continent as being made up of one mass of land, and therefore view Asia and Europe as a single continent, called Eurasia.

AFRO-EURASIA

EURASIA

Africa is connected to Asia by land, so some geographers have referred to it as a supercontinent called Afro-Eurasia or Eurafrasia.

Early map

The oldest known world map is from Asia and dates from around 600 B.C.E. It only shows a few territories, all within Asia. It was made in Babylon (now part of modern-day Iraq), which the map places in the center of the world.

Mountains
Ocean
Habban
Urartu
Babylon
Assyria
Ocean
Bit Yakin
Der
Elam
Ocean

Mountains
Urartu
Assyria
Babylon
Babylonia
Der
Elam

The map is a symbolic map of the world rather than a realistic interpretation. It mentions mythical creatures that connect the world to the heavens.

This modern-day map shows the actual locations of the ancient places from the 600 B.C.E. map.

Countries

Not only is Asia the largest continent in the world, but it is also home to the world's largest countries and contains 60 percent of the world's human population.

Transcontinental countries

There are five countries in Asia that also cross over into the continent of Europe. They are Russia, Azerbaijan, Georgia, Kazakhstan, and Turkey. These are called transcontinental countries.

Large and small

Russia is the largest country in the world. Three quarters of it is in Asia, with the remaining quarter in the continent of Europe.

The largest country that lies wholly in Asia is China, covering around 20 percent of Asia's landmass.

The smallest country in Asia is the Maldives. It is made up of a chain of islands in the Indian Ocean.

Many small islands are included in the continent of Asia. Indonesia is made up of over 17,000 mainly tiny islands—more than any other country in the world.

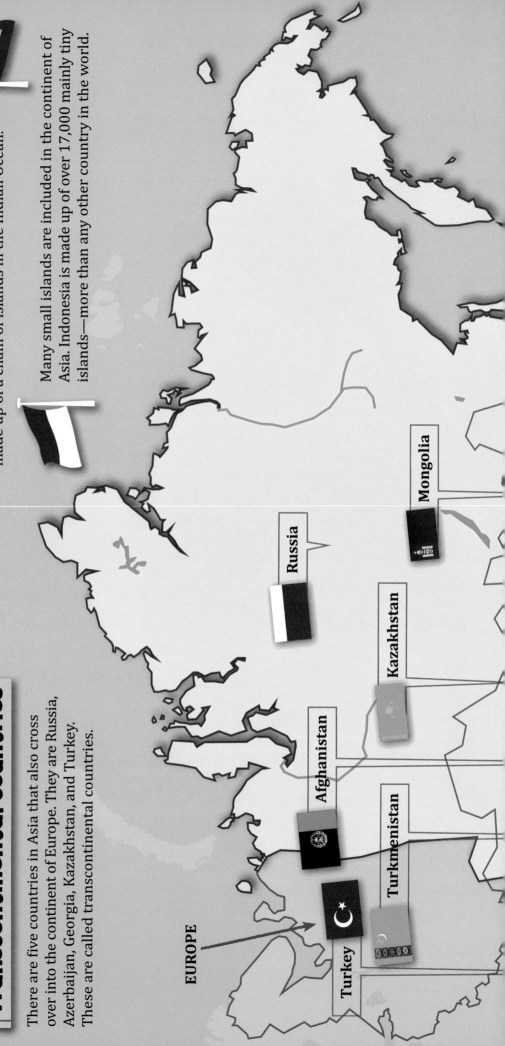

EUROPE

Turkey

Turkmenistan

Afghanistan

Kazakhstan

Russia

Mongolia

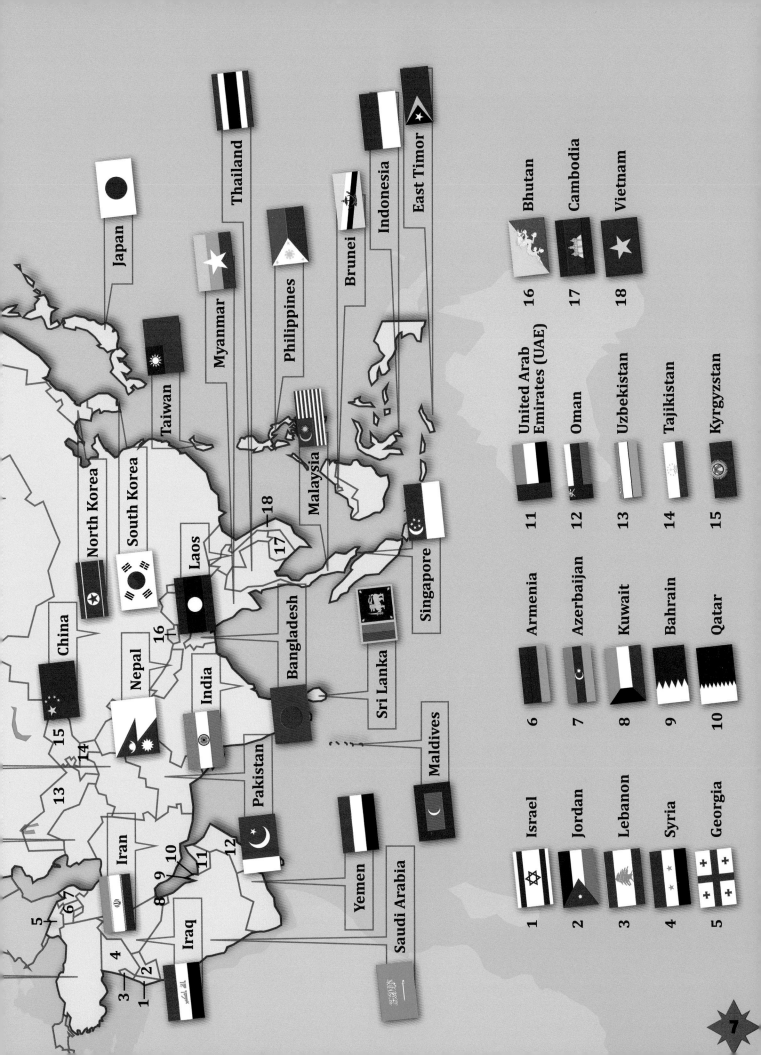

Japan

Thailand

Indonesia

East Timor

Brunei

Myanmar

Philippines

Taiwan

North Korea

South Korea

Laos

Malaysia

Singapore

China

Nepal

India

Bangladesh

Sri Lanka

Maldives

Pakistan

Iran

Iraq

Yemen

Saudi Arabia

16

17

18

11 United Arab Emirates (UAE)

12 Oman

13 Uzbekistan

14 Tajikistan

15 Kyrgyzstan

6 Armenia

7 Azerbaijan

8 Kuwait

9 Bahrain

10 Qatar

1 Israel

2 Jordan

3 Lebanon

4 Syria

5 Georgia

16 Bhutan

17 Cambodia

18 Vietnam

17

18

16

15

14

13

12

11

10

9

8

7

6

5

4

3

2

1

Early civilizations

The term **"civilization"** refers to a complex society, its culture, and way of life that includes centralized cities and communications systems. Many of the world's earliest civilizations began in Asia, where the remains of the first cities and examples of the first writing can still be found today.

Sumerian Civilization 4500–1750 B.C.E.

The Sumerians lived in the southern part of modern-day Iraq, between the Euphrates and Tigris rivers. This region was known as Sumer. Important inventions that have changed the course of history have come from there. These include the invention of the wheel, the first sailing boats, and early forms of writing.

One of the first recorded works of literature is a poem that comes from the Sumerians. It is called the Epic of Gilgamesh and tells the story of Gilgamesh, a king-hero who fights a series of monsters in his search for the secret of eternal life.

The Sumerians built the first cities, building them around giant temples called ziggurats.

What happened to them?

Attackers from Elam, a neighboring area (that is today part of modern-day Iran), ransacked the cities and destroyed Sumer. The land was taken over by Elamites and Amorites from modern-day Syria, followed by other civilizations. Many of the Sumerian cities were left in ruins.

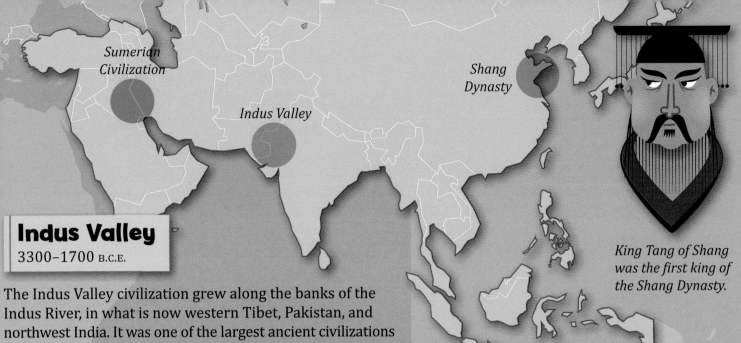

Sumerian
Civilization

Indus Valley

Shang
Dynasty

King Tang of Shang
was the first king of
the Shang Dynasty.

Indus Valley
3300–1700 B.C.E.

The Indus Valley civilization grew along the banks of the
Indus River, in what is now western Tibet, Pakistan, and
northwest India. It was one of the largest ancient civilizations
with more than 1,400 towns and cities. The Indus Valley
people were advanced in urban planning. They designed
cities in a grid pattern, built houses out of solid bricks, and
installed bathrooms with underground plumbing.

Shang Dynasty
1600–1046 B.C.E.

The Shang were a dynasty of kings who ruled
an area of northern China more than 12,000
years ago. Their people were skilled workers
in bronze, bone, ivory, jade, stone, ceramics,
and tortoiseshell. They developed a calendar
and China's first writing system.

Key

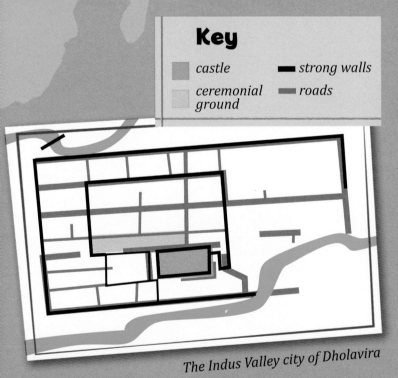

castle
ceremonial
ground
strong walls
roads

The Indus Valley city of Dholavira

The Shang were masters in the art of bronze
casting, and produced elaborately decorated
musical instruments and ceremonial vessels,
as well as weapons such as this ax head.

What happened to them?

No one really knows what caused the end of the
Indus Valley civilization. Some think that
• the land turned to desert, causing people to
starve or move away
• water levels rose along the River Indus, flooding the
land and possibly changing the course of the river
• they faced an invasion by another civilization and
since the Indus people were peaceful, they would not
have survived in battle

What happened
to them?

In the final years of the Shang Dynasty,
there were frequent wars with rival
kingdoms in China. They were finally
defeated in battle by the Zhou Dynasty.

Regions

The countries within Asia are grouped together into regions where they share political, religious, and cultural histories, or a similar location.

Ural Mountains
Northern Asia
Caspian Sea
Central Asia
Black Sea
Aegean Sea
Himalayas
Western Asia
South Asia
Persian Gulf
Mediterranean Sea
Red Sea
Arabian Sea

Northern Asia

Northern Asia is made up of the Asian territory of Russia, east of the Ural Mountains. This area is sometimes referred to by its original name: Siberia.

Central Asia

Central Asia is made up of five countries that all end in "stan," meaning "land of." They are: Kazakhstan, Kyrgyzstan, Tajikistan, Turkmenistan, and Uzbekistan. These countries were part of the Soviet Union until 1991.

Western Asia

Western Asia is surrounded by seven seas: the Aegean Sea, the Black Sea, the Caspian Sea, the Persian Gulf, the Arabian Sea, the Red Sea, and the **Mediterranean** Sea. It includes a region known as the Middle East.

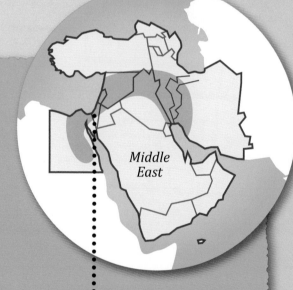

Middle East

The Middle East

The Middle East was originally named by foreign **colonial** powers to distinguish it from nearby India. There are many different peoples and cultures there with different traditions and religions. Islam is the dominant religion.

The Fertile Crescent

Within the Middle East is a region known as the Fertile Crescent. This curved area of land crosses through Iraq, Kuwait, Syria, Lebanon, Jordan, Israel, and into Egypt (in Africa). It is named the Fertile Crescent because the land is perfect for growing crops—a feature that led to it being home to many of the world's first civilizations (see pages 8–9).

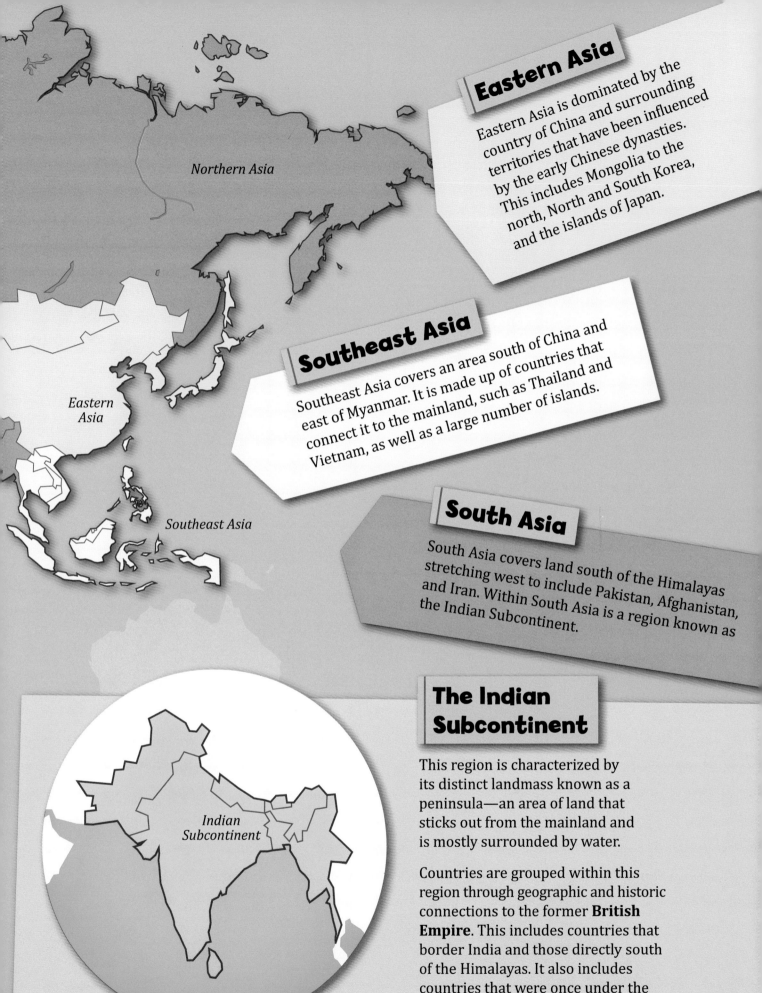

Northern Asia

Eastern Asia

Eastern Asia is dominated by the country of China and surrounding territories that have been influenced by the early Chinese dynasties. This includes Mongolia to the north, North and South Korea, and the islands of Japan.

Eastern Asia

Southeast Asia

Southeast Asia covers an area south of China and east of Myanmar. It is made up of countries that connect it to the mainland, such as Thailand and Vietnam, as well as a large number of islands.

Southeast Asia

South Asia

South Asia covers land south of the Himalayas stretching west to include Pakistan, Afghanistan, and Iran. Within South Asia is a region known as the Indian Subcontinent.

Indian Subcontinent

The Indian Subcontinent

This region is characterized by its distinct landmass known as a peninsula—an area of land that sticks out from the mainland and is mostly surrounded by water.

Countries are grouped within this region through geographic and historic connections to the former **British Empire**. This includes countries that border India and those directly south of the Himalayas. It also includes countries that were once under the colonial control of British India, such as Bhutan and Myanmar.

Climates

Asia sits within the Arctic Circle and the tropics. As a result, the continent is home to some of the coldest and hottest places in the world, as well as some of the driest and wettest.

Asia's climate zones:

- polar
- subarctic
- highland
- humid continental
- Mediterranean
- dry
- tropical

Contrasting climates

The polar **climate** in the north of Russia creates treeless plains, where the soil is permanently frozen. In contrast, the heat and humidity of the tropical climate in the south of Asia helps dense rain forests thrive.

HIMALAYAS

Wettest place on Earth

Mawsynram, a town in India, is known to be the wettest place on Earth. In this part of northeast India, rainclouds get trapped by the world's highest mountain range, the Himalayas, and are unable to escape farther north.

Tirat Tsvi, Israel, has the highest recorded temperature in Asia, with a record high of 129 degrees Fahrenheit (53.9 °C).

Aden, in Yemen, is the driest place in Asia. It receives on average only 1.6 inches (40 mm) of rain each year.

Mawsynram receives more than 39 feet (11.9 m) of rain each year.

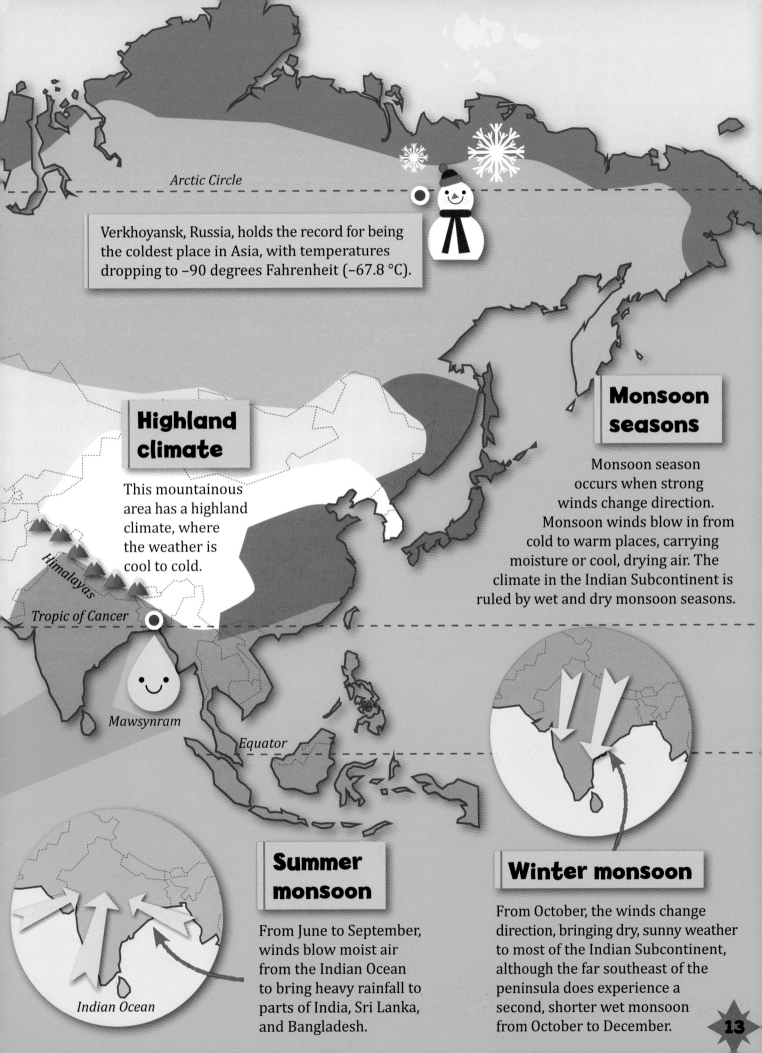

Arctic Circle

Verkhoyansk, Russia, holds the record for being the coldest place in Asia, with temperatures dropping to –90 degrees Fahrenheit (–67.8 °C).

Highland climate

This mountainous area has a highland climate, where the weather is cool to cold.

Himalayas

Tropic of Cancer

Mawsynram

Equator

Monsoon seasons

Monsoon season occurs when strong winds change direction. Monsoon winds blow in from cold to warm places, carrying moisture or cool, drying air. The climate in the Indian Subcontinent is ruled by wet and dry monsoon seasons.

Winter monsoon

From October, the winds change direction, bringing dry, sunny weather to most of the Indian Subcontinent, although the far southeast of the peninsula does experience a second, shorter wet monsoon from October to December.

Summer monsoon

From June to September, winds blow moist air from the Indian Ocean to bring heavy rainfall to parts of India, Sri Lanka, and Bangladesh.

Indian Ocean

Wildlife

Many strange and beautiful animals and plants can only be found living wild in Asia. Hiding in mountain forests or roaming freely on islands and open plains, many of these creatures have become symbols of their region.

Camels

There are two species of camels: the Bactrian camel, which has two humps, and the dromedary camel, which has one hump. Both of these animals can be found in Asia. Camels store fat in their humps, which can be converted into energy and water when no food supplies are available. This makes them the perfect animal for long journeys across deserts.

While most camels in Asia are used for transporting goods, there are some Bactrian camels living wild in the Gobi Desert, across Mongolia and China.

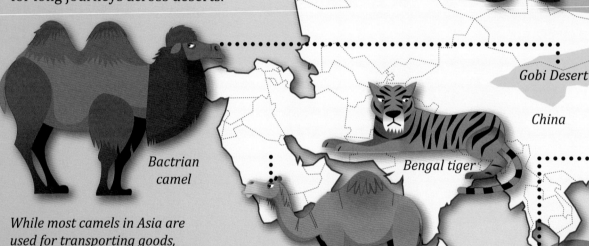

Bactrian camel

Dromedary camel

Arctic hare

Brown bear

Gobi Desert

China

Bengal tiger

Sumatran rhinoceros

Borneo

Sumatra

Komodo dragon

The Komodo dragon is the world's largest lizard and only lives wild on five Indonesian islands. They can grow almost 10 feet (3 m) in length and weigh more than 300 pounds (136 kg). They feast on animals ranging in size from small mice to large water buffaloes.

Flores

Rinca

Komodo

Gili Motang

Gili Dasami

Taiga forest

The taiga forest in Russia is one of the largest forested areas in the world. It makes up around one half of the world's evergreen forests. It is also one of the coldest areas of Asia. Animals that live here, such as Arctic hares, grow thick fur coats to help them survive the harsh winter months.

Bamboo

Bamboo is one of the fastest growing plants in the world. Some bamboo can grow as much as 3 feet (1 m) in 24 hours! Bamboo plants can also grow very tall, some reaching 115 feet (35 m) in height.

Bamboo is an important plant for the economy in East and Southeast Asia. It's used as a building material, for food, for making furniture, and even for bamboo bikes and skateboards.

Rafflesia arnoldii

The rafflesia arnoldii is the largest known flower in the world. It can grow up to 3.3 feet (1 m) across. The flower is also one of the nastiest smelling, perfuming the air with the smell of rotting meat.

Giant panda

The giant panda is an **endangered** species. There are only around 1,600 left in the wild.

Giant pandas live mainly in bamboo forests high in the mountains of western China. Their diet is approximately 99 percent bamboo. They can eat up to 31 pounds (14 kg) of bamboo shoots a day—and poo up to 40 times a day!

Orangutan

Orangutans are found in the tropical rain forests of Sumatra and Borneo. The name orangutan means "man of the forest" in the Malay language. They are dependent on the forest for shelter and food, spending around 90 percent of their time up in the trees.

Natural landmarks

The broad landscape of Asia contains the world's highest mountains, large deserts, and amazing sites of stone forests, white **terraces**, and salty lakes.

The Dead Sea

The Dead Sea is between Israel and Jordan. Although it's called a sea, it's really a lake, with water flowing into it from the Jordan River.

The Dead Sea is also known as the Salt Sea. There is so much salt in the water that people can easily float on it.

Sea level

The Dead Sea is the lowest spot on Earth's land surface, at 1,368 feet (417 m) below sea level.

The Himalayas

The Himalayas are a mountain range that crosses through Pakistan, India, China, Nepal, and Bhutan. It's the highest mountain range on Earth, containing 9 out of 10 of the world's highest peaks, including Mount Everest—the world's highest mountain.

Cho Oyu
26,906 feet
(8,201 m)

Everest
29,029 feet
(8,848 m)

Lhotse
27,939 feet
(8,516 m)

Makalu
27,762 feet
(8,462 m)

Manaslu
26,758 feet
(8,156 m)

A section of the Himalayas

K2 is the second-highest mountain in the world. It is 28,251 feet (8,611 m) high and is located between China and Pakistan in the Karakoram mountain range.

Lake Baikal

Caspian Sea

Mount Fuji

Mount Fuji is a symbol of Japan. It's the country's highest mountain, measuring 12,388 feet (3,776 m). It's also an active volcano, although it last erupted in 1707.

Gobi Desert

The Gobi Desert is a cold, rocky desert and only around 5 percent of it is covered in sand. It is an important area for fossil finds—dinosaur eggs were first discovered there.

The Yangtze River is 3,915 miles (6,300 km) long. It's the longest river in Asia and the third-longest river in the world.

Pamukkale

Pamukkale, meaning "cotton castle" in Turkish, is an area with terraces that appear bright white and foamy. These terraces were created by deposits of calcium carbonate that bubble up from hot springs.

Shilin Stone Forest

In the Yunnan Province of China is an area of land covered with hundreds of tall rocks, some reaching up to 98 feet (30 m) in height. The rocks were carved by more than 270 million years of earthquakes, wind, and water erosion. They look like a dense forest made of stone.

Gobi Desert

Himalayas

Karakum Desert

Thar Desert

Arabian Desert

Human-made landmarks

From the awe-inspiring ancient structures of the past to towering modern-day towers, Asia is home to some of the world's most breathtaking and record-breaking architecture.

City of Petra

The city of Petra in Jordan is made up of temples, tombs, theaters, and houses that are half-built and half-carved into rock. Petra has existed for more than 2,000 years. It is one of the world's largest archaeological sites and is home to the remains of historic Arab and Mediterranean communities.

Burj Khalifa

The Burj Khalifa in Dubai in the United Arab Emirates is the tallest human-made structure in the world. It stands at 2,716 feet (828 m) tall. From the top, you can see all of Dubai and even as far as the neighboring country of Iran.

Historians believe Petra was established as a meeting point for different trade routes, with camels transporting spices and other goods between the Mediterranean, Africa, the Middle East, and India.

Taj Mahal

The Taj Mahal, in the northern city of Agra, is the most popular tourist attraction in India. It was built between 1631 and 1648 for the grief-stricken **Mughal** emperor Shah Jahan, as a tomb for his third and favorite wife, Mumtaz Mahal.

The four sides of the building appear identical with a repeated pattern of large arches and domes.

The building is made from white marble that appears to change color at different times of the day.

Great Wall of China

The Great Wall of China is the world's longest wall, stretching across China for 13,171 miles (21,196 km). It was built by many different emperors over a long time period to keep out invaders.

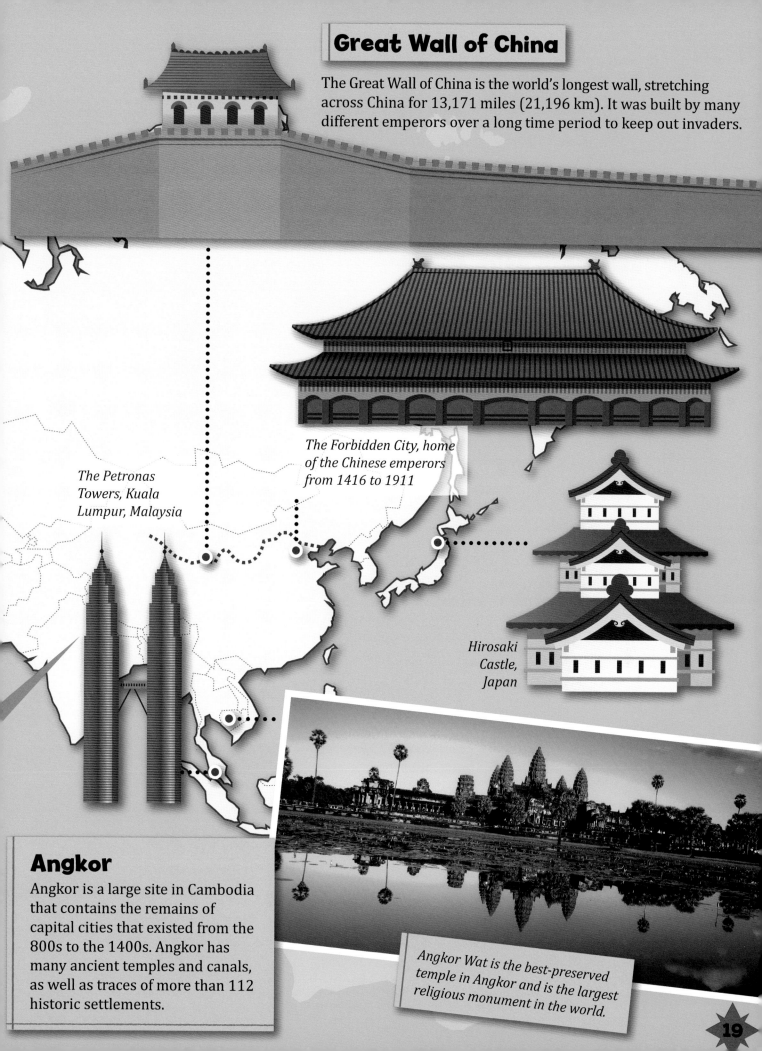

The Forbidden City, home of the Chinese emperors from 1416 to 1911

The Petronas Towers, Kuala Lumpur, Malaysia

Hirosaki Castle, Japan

Angkor

Angkor is a large site in Cambodia that contains the remains of capital cities that existed from the 800s to the 1400s. Angkor has many ancient temples and canals, as well as traces of more than 112 historic settlements.

Angkor Wat is the best-preserved temple in Angkor and is the largest religious monument in the world.

Industries

More than half of the population of Asia earns a living through farming. Manufacturing and fuel industries are also big employers, with large companies and resources supplying the continent—and the rest of the world—with energy, clothing and textiles, and electronics.

Main industries in Asia

Crops:
- Rice
- Sugar
- Tea
- Fruit
- Wheat
- Cotton

Industries:
- Manufacturing/Industrial Areas
- Forestry
- High tech
- Fishing
- Textiles
- Tourism

Livestock:
- Cattle
- Sheep
- Pigs

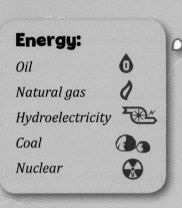

Energy:
- Oil
- Natural gas
- Hydroelectricity
- Coal
- Nuclear

Oil and gas

At least 60 percent of the world's known oil and gas deposits are found in Asia, most notably the oil fields of the Persian Gulf. The discovery of oil there in the 1930s brought great wealth to countries with a Persian Gulf coastline: Iran, Saudi Arabia, United Arab Emirates (UAE), Kuwait, Qatar, and Bahrain. Combined, these countries supply one fifth of the world with oil.

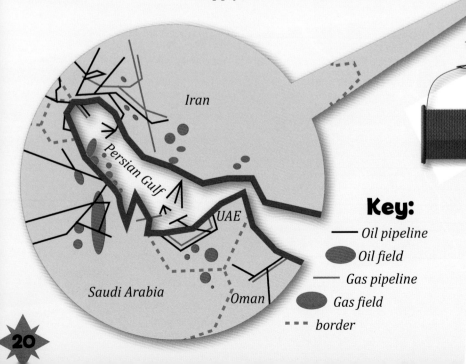

Iran

Persian Gulf

UAE

Saudi Arabia

Oman

Key:
— Oil pipeline
⬭ Oil field
— Gas pipeline
⬭ Gas field
- - - border

Textiles

The textile industry is key to the economies and employment of workers in India and Bangladesh. They are two of the world's biggest textile **exporters**.

78 percent of Bangladesh's export earnings come from textiles

India has more land set aside for growing cotton than any other country in the world

Rice farming

The most important crop in Asia is rice. More than 90 percent of the world's rice is produced and consumed there. The Chinese people grow and eat the most rice in the world, followed by the people of India, Indonesia, Bangladesh, Vietnam, Philippines, and Myanmar.

Most rice is grown in paddy fields; these are human-made ponds that are built into the landscape often in terraces, or steps, in steep hillsides.

Electronics

At the end of the 1990s, Japan was the number-one country for manufacturing electronic goods. It introduced the handheld camcorder, CD player, and Nintendo Game Boy. However, South Korea has begun to steal Japan's position as the top exporter of electronic goods. South Korea is home to Samsung Electronics, the world's largest technology company and largest manufacturer of cell phones.

Hydroelectricity

Three Gorges Dam

Hydroelectricity produces electricity through the gravitational force of falling or flowing water

Dams channel and direct the force of water

The water turns turbines, which then generate electricity

Hydroelectricity is a type of renewable energy and accounts for around 16 percent of the world's electricity. China is the world's largest producer and has the world's largest hydroelectric power station: the Three Gorges Dam. Built on the Yangtze River, the dam stretches about 0.8 miles (1.3 km) across and is 594 feet (181 m) high.

21

Settlements

Asia is the most populated continent in the world. It's estimated that three out of every five people on Earth live in Asia. While there are many large areas of land and islands where hardly anyone lives, most of the population is crammed into urban areas, with Asia being home to the world's most overcrowded cities.

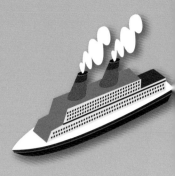

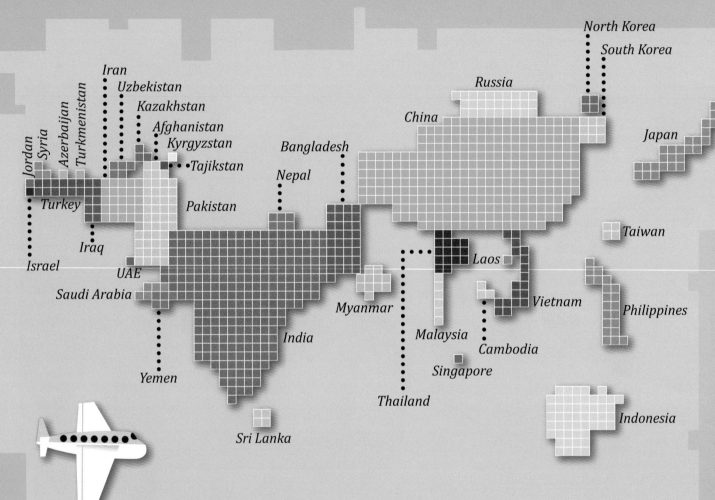

Population map

This is a population map of Asia, where the size of each country is shown in proportion to its population. Each square represents 5 million people; countries with a population of fewer than 5 million are not shown. This map makes China appear as the largest country, even though it is smaller in size than Russia.

Palm Island, United Arab Emirates

Palm Island is attached to the mainland of Dubai, in the United Arab Emirates. It's an artificial island constructed from sand dredged up from the bottom of the Persian Gulf, shaped like a palm tree with a surrounding crescent. The island took five years to build, was completed in 2006, and measures 3.1 miles by 3.1 miles (5 km by 5 km).

Mongolia

One third of Mongolians live in the capital city Ulan Bator, while the rest inhabit smaller urban areas or farmland. Historically, Mongolians were a **nomadic** people who roamed freely across the land. A small minority still live this way, moving across the vast western area of grassland and shrubland, known as the **steppes**. They herd cattle and live in tents called **gers**. In the past, gers were moved from place to place with ox and carts. Today, they are transported on trucks.

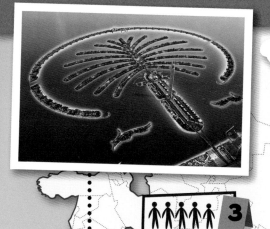

Ger

five million people

Megacities

A megacity is an urban area with a population of more than 10 million. Out of the top ten largest megacities in the world, nine are Asian. The largest cities in Asia are:

 1 Tokyo, Japan, 37.8 million people   **4** Manila, Philippines, 24.1 million people

 2 Jakarta, Indonesia, 30.5 million people   **5** Seoul, South Korea, 23.48 million people

 3 Delhi, India, 24.9 million people

Tokyo skyline

23

Sports

In countries across Asia, people are passionate about a wide variety of sports, some of which are unique to a country or region. Many sports played in Asia have their roots in history and specific cultures.

Martial arts

Eastern Asia is home to many of the world's most well-known and popular martial arts. Although more commonly seen as a set of skills for self-defence, competitions, and action-movie fight scenes, many of the martial arts developed out of ancient philosophies. They have a focus on spiritual and mental development that is still valued today.

Kendo

Japan is home to martial arts that are popular all over the world, such as judo and karate. It's also the country where kendo comes from. Kendo means "way of the sword" and has developed over 1,000 years. Opponents fight each other using a bamboo sword called a shinai, while dressed in protective armor.

A rei, or bow, is performed before a kendo combat begins

Rhythmic gymnastics

The most popular sport for girls in Russia is rhythmic gymnastics. This sport involves an individual or small team performing a routine that combines elements of ballet, gymnastics, and dance. The routines usually involve an apparatus such as a ball, hoop, or ribbon.

Camel racing

Camel racing has existed in Arab countries since around 600 C.E., but became a professional sport only within the last 100 years. United Arab Emirates is the center of camel racing in Asia, housing top training grounds with treadmills and swimming pools to exercise their highly prized racing camels.

Taekwondo

Taekwondo is the national sport of South Korea. The name Taekwondo breaks down to mean (*Tae*) foot, (*Kwon*) hand, (*Do*) art. The hands and feet are mainly used to overcome an opponent.

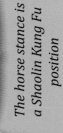

Taekwondo move: flying side kick

Shaolin Kung Fu

Shaolin Kung Fu has existed for more than 1,500 years and was originally practiced by Buddhist monks in the Henan province of China. It began as a series of exercises built around **meditation** and developed into skills used for self-defence.

The horse stance is a Shaolin Kung Fu position

Jakarta

Cricket

Cricket is more popular in India and Pakistan than anywhere else in the world. It was introduced to the area by the British in the 1700s. Both countries produce some of the world's greatest cricket players.

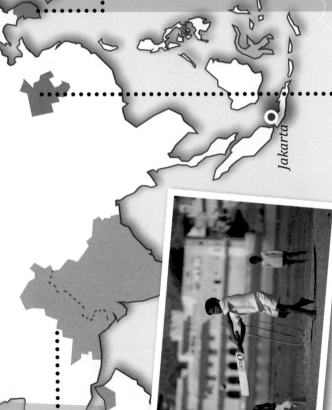

Asian Games

The Asian Games take place once every four years, with 45 nations from the continent competing in a number of different sports, including swimming, table tennis, and basketball. It's the second-largest multi-sporting event in the world, next to the Olympic Games. The first Asian Games took place in New Delhi, India, in 1951. The next games will be held in 2018, in Jakarta, Indonesia.

113

25

Culture

Many of the world's largest religions trace their beginnings to Asia, and many Asian cities have strong cultural connections to different faiths. The continent is known for its often spectacular cultural events and celebrations.

Judaism

Judaism, the religion of the Jews, began more than 3,500 years ago, in a place called Canaan. This was once a large country that covered parts of present-day Lebanon, Syria, Jordan, and Israel.

Lebanon
Syria
CANAAN
Israel
Iraq
Jordan
Saudi Arabia
Egypt

Russian ballet

Ballet is popular throughout all of Russia. The Russian State Ballet is based in its Asian territory, Krasnoyarsk.

Krasnoyarsk

Islam

It's traditionally thought that Islam began in 610 C.E., when the archangel Jibril visited the **Prophet Muhammad** on the Jabal al-Nour mountain near Mecca.

Sikhism

Sikhism was founded in the Punjab province of northern India in the 1400s, by the teachings of Guru Nanak.

Varanasi

Christianity

Christianity began more than 2,000 years ago with the birth of Jesus Christ in Bethlehem, in the present-day Palestinian area of Israel.

Buddhism

Buddhism originated in northeast India in the 500s B.C.E., beginning with the birth of Buddha.

The Grand Mosque in Mecca

Mecca

Mecca, or Makkah, in Saudi Arabia is the birthplace of the Prophet Muhammad—the founder of Islam. Wherever they are in the world, Muslims always pray facing Mecca. All Muslims are required to make a **pilgrimage** there at least once in their lifetime.

Hinduism

Varanasi is one of the most sacred sites for Hinduism, the dominant religion of India. Varanasi is often called the holy city of India. It's home to more than 20,000 temples, **shrines**, and other places of worship. It has importance for Buddhism, too. It's believed that its founder, Buddha, began preaching near the city.

Varanasi is one of the oldest continually inhabited cities. It dates back to 1000–1100 B.C.E.

Chinese New Year

Chinese New Year is a major festival and holiday in China, and is also celebrated around the world in cities and countries where there are large Chinese populations. The celebrations begin at the turn of the Chinese calendar and last for 15 days.

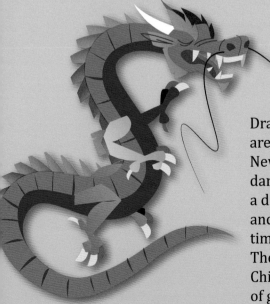

Dragon dances are popular at New Year, with dancers holding a dragon aloft and moving it in time with music. The dragon is a Chinese symbol of good luck.

Shadow puppets

Shadow puppetry is popular in many Southeast Asian countries. The puppets have intricate designs with moveable body parts. They are held behind a white cloth, with a light shining behind to cast a shadow onto the cloth. The puppets are used to act out religious stories and folktales.

Food and drink

Asian cuisine is popular all over the world, with Chinese restaurants, Indian curry houses, and Japanese sushi bars attracting hungry people. Often the ingredients of traditional recipes have been altered to suit local tastes and preferences, but the more traditional dishes can still be found in Asia.

Asian takeout

SWEET AND SOUR PORK

One of the most popular Chinese dishes eaten around the world is sweet and sour pork. The sauce originates from the Canton province of Southern China. The ingredients include sugar that makes it sweet, and rice vinegar that provides the sour taste.

VINDALOO CURRY

The curries that are eaten in Asia, from countries such as India and Thailand, are often very different from those eaten in Asian restaurants outside of the continent. Chicken, shrimp, or lamb vindaloo is often the spiciest dish on a restaurant menu. But in Goa, in India, where it originated, it is less spicy and is mainly served with pork.

SUSHI

Sushi is the name for a Japanese dish made of small amounts of cold rice flavored with vinegar. The rice is often wrapped in seaweed and topped with seafood, fish, or vegetables, or wrapped around fish and vegetables.

SUMMER ROLLS

A popular appetizer from Vietnam is the summer roll, also known as a salad roll. The rolls are full of shrimp, bits of pork, vegetables, and rice noodles, all wrapped together in rice paper "rolls." It is often served with chili, peanut, or sweet soy dipping sauces.

Tea

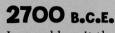

After water, tea is the most widely consumed beverage in the world. The majority of the tea today comes from countries in Asia, such as India, Sri Lanka, and Indonesia. The largest producer of tea is China, where the history of tea drinking begins...

2700 B.C.E.
Legend has it that Chinese Emperor Shen Nong accidentally invented tea. While he sat under a *camellia sinensis* tree, some leaves are believed to have fallen into his cup of hot water.

900 C.E.
Tea drinking spreads to Japan, where the tea ceremony is created. The ceremony involves **rituals** around preparing the tea and the space in which one drinks it. These may vary depending on local customs, but the aim is to achieve a peaceful and serene experience.

300 B.C.E.
Tea becomes a daily drink in China.

1800s
British colonizers establish tea **plantations** in India. Today, India is the second largest producer of tea, behind China.

1600s
Tea reaches Europe.

1980s
Bubble tea was invented in Taiwan in the 1980s, but has only recently become popular around the world. This drink mixes tea with fruit juice or milk and contains either jellies or balls of tapioca. The drink is mostly served cold and is shaken to create frothy bubbles.

Further information

COUNTRY	SIZE SQ MI*	POPULATION	CAPITAL CITY	MAIN LANGUAGES
China	3,705,405.5	1,367,485,388	Beijing	Mandarin Chinese
India	1,269,218.8	1,251,695,584	New Delhi	Hindi, Bengali, English
Indonesia	735,357.9	255,993,674	Jakarta	Indonesian
Pakistan	307,373.9	199,085,847	Islamabad	Urdu, Punjabi, English
Bangladesh	57,320.7	168,957,745	Dhaka	Bengali
Russia	6,601,665.4 [including European territory]	142,423,773 [whole country]	Moscow	Russian
Japan	145,913.7	126,919,659	Tokyo	Japanese
Philippines	115,830.6	100,998,376	Manila	Filipino, English
Vietnam	127,880.8	94,348,835	Hanoi	Vietnamese
Iran	636,371.4	81,824,270	Tehran	Persian
Turkey	302,534.9 [including European territory]	79,414,269 [whole country]	Ankara	Turkish
Thailand	198,116.7	67,976,405	Bangkok	Thai
Myanmar	261,228.1	56,320,206	Naypyidaw	Burmese
South Korea	38,502.1	49,115,196	Seoul	Korean
Iraq	169,235.1	37,056,169	Baghdad	Arabic, Kurdish
Afghanistan	251,827.3	32,564,342	Kabul	Dari, Pashto
Nepal	56,826.9	31,551,305	Kathmandu	Nepali
Malaysia	127,354.6	30,513,848	Kuala Lumpur	Malay
Uzbekistan	172,742	29,199,942	Tashkent	Uzbek
Saudi Arabia	829,999.6	27,752,316	Riyadh	Arabic
Yemen	203,849.5	26,737,317	Sana'a	Arabic
North Korea	46,540	24,983,205	Pyongyang	Korean
Taiwan	13,892	23,415,126	Taipei	Mandarin Chinese
Sri Lanka	25,332.2	22,053,488	Sri Jayawardenepura Kotte, Colombo	Sinhala, Tamil
Kazakhstan	1,052,089 [including European territory]	18,157,122 [whole country]	Astana	Kazakh, Russian
Syria	71,498.4	17,064,854	Damascus	Arabic
Cambodia	69,898	15,708,756	Phnom Penh	Khmer
Azerbaijan	33,436.4 [including European territory]	9,780,780 [whole country]	Baku	Azerbaijani
Tajikistan	144,100	8,191,958	Dushanbe	Tajik
Jordan	34,495.1	8,117,564	Amman	Arabic
Israel	8,019.3	8,049,314	Jerusalem	Hebrew, Arabic
Laos	91,429	6,911,544	Vientiane	Lao
Lebanon	4,015.4	6,184,701	Beirut	Arabic
United Arab Emirates	32,278.1	5,779,760	Abu Dhabi	Arabic
Singapore	269.1	5,674,472	Singapore	Mandarin, English, Malay
Kyrgyzstan	77,201.5	5,664,939	Bishkek	Kyrgyz, Russian
Turkmenistan	188,456.4	5,231,422	Ashgabat	Turkmen
Georgia	26,911.3 [including European territory]	4,931,226 [whole country]	Tbilisi	Georgian
Oman	119,498.6	3,286,936	Muscat	Arabic
Armenia	11,483.8	3,056,382	Yerevan	Armenian
Mongolia	603,908.3	2,992,908	Ulaanbaatar	Mongolian
Kuwait	6,879.6	2,788,534	Kuwait City	Arabic
Qatar	4,473.4	2,194,817	Doha	Arabic
Bahrain	293.4	1,346,613	Manama	Arabic
East Timor	5,742.9	1,231,116	Dili	Portuguese, Tetum
Bhutan	14,824	741,919	Thimphu	Dzongkha
Brunei	2,225.9	429,646	Bandar Seri Begawan	Malay
Maldives	115.1	393,253	Malé	Dhivehi

*To arrive at square kilometers (sq km), divide a number in square miles (sq mi) by 0.386102.

Glossary

British Empire
An empire is a group of countries governed under a single authority, such as under one ruler or country. The British Empire was comprised of the colonies and other territories ruled by the United Kingdom between the 1500s and 1900s.

civilization
a community that is well organized, with advanced cities, political structures, and often written or codified languages

climate
average weather conditions in a particular area

colonial
relating to the colonies—countries or areas controlled by another country and occupied by settlers from that country

endangered
at risk of extinction, or dying out

equator
an imaginary line drawn around Earth separating the Northern and Southern hemispheres

exporters
a person, business, or country that sells goods to another country

gers
circular tents built with a framework of poles covered in felt or animal skins, used by nomadic people in Mongolia

meditation
spending time in quiet thought for religious purposes, concentration, or relaxation

Mughal
an empire that ruled over parts of South Asia from the 1500s to the 1700s; It was known for its art, architecture, and centralized government

nomadic
roaming from place to place; describing the lifestyle of people and tribes who live in no fixed place, but move their homes around different parts of their country

pilgrimage
a journey to a special place, such as a site of religious importance

plantations
areas where one specific crop is grown on a large scale

prophet
someone who is said to have been in contact with a god and delivers that god's knowledge to followers of a religion

rituals
acts that are always performed in the same sequence, often as a ceremony that has spiritual or religious significance

shrine
a place or monument that is connected to religion and where people visit to perform an act of worship

steppes
large areas of unforested grassland

terraces
a series of flat areas on a slope or hillside that are formed or built like steep steps

Index